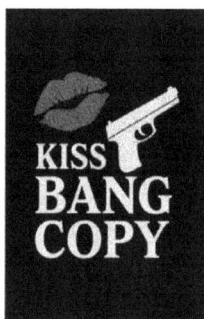

KISS
BANG
COPY

For Mad Maggie Mack

# 1.

Bill Tucker watched the dark water moving below his feet.

He sat on top of a wooden pylon, part of the now defunct city docks. The docks were once a big and powerful lifeline to the city. No life now though; the docks sat quiet, rotting and surplus to the city's needs. Bill Tucker and this dockyard shared their lives. The dockyard was dead, and Bill was heading the same way. All it took was for him to push off the pylon and land in the icy water. The only witness would be the moon, whose reflection he would aim for. He could sink into the icy darkness and be gone.

It wouldn't take too long.

His thoughts were whirling like the cold wind around him, bringing dirt and dust to the surface. His thoughts were low as he thought about how time eased on, and nothing changed. He hadn't changed. Eventually, as he had a hundred times before, he turned around and stepped back onto the wharf, leaving his thoughts of suicide behind. He had been sitting for so long his legs felt rubbery as he walked away from the water's edge. His head stayed low on his chest as he made his way through the familiar docklands. His thoughts had run the gamut of where he was in life – what he was doing ... where he was going. He steered his mind away from the dark and negative as he walked out.

He walked slowly, without any real purpose, his hands thrust deep in the pockets of his old jacket. There was nothing for him to rush to, no one to see. Just his small box of an apartment and the cockroaches he shared it with. He walked past the old mess-room with its boarded-up windows and doors nailed shut, through to the abandoned security office. The gate had been padlocked years ago, but time and corrosion had pressured the fence and gates to create gaps. The bent poles and aged sagging wire had parted through decades of neglect so that a guy of Bill's large size could get through without effort.

The familiar, empty streets held no interest as he passed trashed cars and broken fixtures. Arc lights painted the surroundings in an orange hue. From the other side of the harbour, Bill could see the glass building glittering like stars in a distant universe. Tenancies on this side of town hadn't heard of gentrification yet. The old brickwork reflected the people stacked inside, one upon the other, connected by mud if connected at all.

Bill arrived at the concrete steps that led into his building. It was the same as the others in the block. Five floors of people he didn't know. Once he had known tenants and neighbours, but during various drinking binges he had upset them for one reason or another. One thing he had in common with his neighbours was that everyone had the same posture. Head down and minding their own business. Everyone had eyes, but no one used them. He walked up the stairs without grabbing the iron railing that divided the entrance walkway and passed through the aluminium doors into the stark white of overhead fluorescence.

The building manager was standing in the foyer. He knew her and nodded hello, but she didn't respond. A thin old lady with a sharp wit and scary eyes, she stood there staring with concern up the staircase, her cigarette held high in front of her face, ready for the next drag.

Bill walked by and up the stairs. At the second level, he saw what the building manager lady must have been waiting for. There were two men in dark suits outside apartment 2B. One man was leaning on the opposite wall looking through the open door. The other man was leaning in the door frame talking to the occupant.

Bill knew who they were. These guys had been in the building before. They were the guys that came to kick people out who hadn't paid up. They worked for the local crime boss who owned the building. These were his enforcers. Bad men with short tempers. If they don't get what they want, they usually ended up cracking something open, like the head of the person who wouldn't leave. There had been more than one occasion where Bill had followed a blood trail down the stairs when going for his morning walk.

He didn't know who lived in 2B. He didn't care either, but for what it was worth, he didn't want to see the guy have his head split open. Bill watched for a moment. He should go home. Just leave. It was not his concern or worry. He turned his feet to walk up the stairs, but his mind stayed. Home to what? There was no one there. He didn't have a TV. He didn't even have a radio.

The guy leaning on the wall noticed Bill and shook his head, pulling back his jacket, showing the handle of a gun tucked in his pants. The international warning of 'Go away or we will hurt you'.

Bill's brain popped into gear. That warning had spurred Bill into action. He stepped off the landing and walked towards the door.

The guy stepped into the middle of the hallway, 'Hey,' he said.

'Are you trying to get him out?' Bill asked.

'Yeah, and we aren't trying, we *will* get him out.'

Bill brought his hands up defensively, 'Allow me to help,' he said.

The guy thought for a moment, gave Bill the up and down, acknowledging his size and smirked in self-amusement. 'Sure, give it a go. Sully, get out of the way. This giant is going to help us.'

The guy leaning in the doorway looked over his shoulder and stepped back, wide eyed at the unexpected sight of Bill standing next to him. 'Are you sure?' he asked.

'Yeah, why not,' said the first guy. 'It can't do any harm. It may make things easier.'

Sully stepped back and laughed, 'Okay.'

The two men exchanged amused glances at the sudden change in their routine.

Bill stepped into the tiny room, filling the space. It was the same as his except the curtains were black. His curtains were red. Sitting on a single bed, next to a small table with an alarm clock and an ashtray with four unused syringes resting like cigarettes, was a thin, sweaty man, with unwashed hair. He looked about thirty years old which, in junky years, meant he was probably in his twenties. The skin on the man's face was pulled tight against his skull, his jaundiced eyes darted around in their sockets like they were looking for somewhere to rest but couldn't land anywhere.

'Are you leaving?' Bill asked.

'I'm not fucking leaving. This is my home, man.'

'It's time to go.' Bill peered over his shoulder at the two guys at the door. 'Grab your stash and go now. I live here too. Don't mess with these guys. Whatever its worth, it's not worth it.'

The man paused, getting the message from an equal. 'Okay, okay,' he said and reached under the bed. But instead of a stash of drugs, he came out with a hunting knife and slashed it towards Bill's stomach. Surprised, Bill stepped back, and the knife missed him. In a reflex action, Bill slapped the man as hard as he could. The motion was fast, and the slap connected with a sickening wet sound. The man spun backwards and landed on the bed, dropping the knife, a stunned look on his face.

Bill peered behind him again. The two men were standing there with hands on their guns but neither had drawn, their faces impassive. There was a plastic bag on the floor in the corner, and Bill picked it up, grabbed whatever possessions were in the room and dropped them in, including the large knife and the four syringes from the ashtray. He grabbed the man off the bed by his arm and walked him to the door.

The two guys stepped back, allowing Bill to push the thin man out into the corridor. The thin man looked at Bill. 'Thanks a lot, I think you knocked a tooth out.'

'It wouldn't have been long out anyway. At least you're not bleeding,' Bill said, releasing his arm and dropping the bag to the ground.

Sully stepped forward and closed the door to 2B, locking it. 'This guy just did you a favour; you should thank him.'

'Fuck you,' he said, picked up the bag and stomped off towards the stairs.

Bill shrugged and slowly followed him.

'Hey,' Sully called, 'What's your name?'

Bill turned back. 'Bill,' he said.

'Thanks, Bill.'

Bill turned away and walked up to his room. That night he cooked canned soup and ate it looking out the window of his bedsit towards the brick wall and a window that had never opened on the opposite building, three-and-a-half metres away. It was the same building, housing the same people, doing the same thing. At least Bill had a window; he was glad for that. One day someone might open that other window. Maybe they would talk to each other.

*** 

The next morning, Bill was sitting in the same spot, watching the opposite window, when there was a knock on his door – an unexpected event that hadn't happened for two or three years. Bill walked over, opened the door a little and peeked out. Sully stood there, suit and tie, gun poking out of his pants. Bill opened the door all the way.

'Hey,' Sully said.

'I have paid for this month,' Bill said, unsure of himself.

'No, I am not here for that. Do you want to earn some money today?'

## 2.

The car was big, roomy, a new type of SUV. Bill hadn't been in a car for a long time, and he liked this one. It fitted him. Or he fitted it, more accurately. His shoulders weren't compressed against the side, and he had leg room. His head didn't touch the roof. Sitting next to the man called Sully was the other man from the corridor. Bill didn't know his name.

They drove for twenty-five minutes before arriving in a lane. Bill wasn't sure where they were. It was an industrial area with small factories and workshops lined up close and tight. It was an old part of town, worn and tired, but still functional with life. Not like where he lived. In this part of town, trucks came and went after being loaded or unloaded by ancient forklifts. Hot, orange welding sparks flew out of doors to die on the footpath. Liquids made their escape down cracked concrete driveways to pool in colourful swirls in the worn and crushed concrete curb.

They stopped in a dark, narrow street and parked behind a delivery van with the back doors open. For some reason, the two men appeared to move in slow motion as they got out of the car.

Bill sat for a moment, unsure what to do, and then followed suit. He got out and stood behind the other guy until Sully rounded the front of the car. 'Wait here for a minute, will you, Bill? Charlie and I are going inside for a minute.' They walked to the door of the factory, looked at each other and nodded as confirmation of readiness, then Sully went through the door first, moving to the left, followed by Charlie to the right, in what looked like a choreographed move.

Having been given some instruction, Bill relaxed a little. Since being picked up this morning, he wasn't sure what was expected of him. Sully and Charlie – he now knew the guy's name – had a coffee and a danish pastry waiting in the car for him. Bill had scoffed his quickly, enjoying the treat immensely but made a bit of a mess in the back seat. Sully and Charlie didn't seem to mind and had a laugh at his expense as they sipped their own coffees. Bill had sat back and enjoyed the drive in the nice new car, looking forward to seeing what the fuss was about.

Sully and Charlie returned stone-faced and serious. Sully approached Bill. 'Bill, can you go inside, turn to the left and you'll find a small office. In that office, there is a fat man with a strange coat. Can you convince him to come outside for a chat?'

Bill stared at him, then at Charlie.

'Just get him out here,' Charlie said.

Bill headed towards the door thinking it was a strange request but didn't seem too difficult. Inside, a dark cavern opened up to reveal high industrial pallet racking with black dust covering everything. An old brown Bundy clock hung on the wall like a spiritual carving, a reminder to all, that time is what matters. *Punch in, punch out. See you tomorrow.* Bill understood this philosophy. He wondered where all the workers were as he wandered through cold-steel and resting machinery. It was like the docks where he once worked.

He ducked his head slightly to walk into the open doorway of an ancient office. Threadbare carpet marked a path to a wooden desk covered in papers and folders. Pictures of naked women and motorbikes lined the walls to cover the wood panelling. Behind a desk sat a man, wearing a jacket with studs around the collar. He had a thick neck and long black hair like an aged rocker.

Bill looked at the man, the man looked at Bill. 'Who the fuck are you?' the man said.

'I'm Bill.' He motioned with his head towards the door. 'They want to talk to you outside.'

The man snarled. 'I fucking know that; that is why I am sitting right fucking here. What business is it of yours anyway?'

Bill shuffled his feet. He finally knew why they had brought him here. He just didn't want to do it. 'They sent me in to ask you to come outside, so they can chat with you.'

'Are you fucking daft? Didn't I just tell you I know that? Tell them to fuck off.'

Bill wasn't sure. He wanted this man to just get up and walk out. He didn't care if the man was upset or walked slow or had a wheelchair or had three fucking legs. As long as he got up and went outside. If the man said no again, he would have to do something physical. 'I need you to come outside with me, please,' Bill said, looking out the doorway towards the daylight.

The man chuckled. 'Get out,' he said and started reading something on his desk.

It was time for action. Bill could feel it in his bones. He stepped up to the front of the desk, like an employee would seeking advice from his boss. He fixed his eyes on the tiny little studs. 'Do they hurt your neck?' he asked.

The man looked up into Bill's face. 'What the fuck are you talking about?'

Bill said, 'The studs on your jacket; do they scratch you?'

The man laughed. 'No, for fuck's—'

Bill swiped with his right hand, the slap connecting just below the man's ear. His head snapped sideways, and he flipped out of the chair onto the ground.

'... Fuck me. What the fuck?'

Bill walked around the desk and picked up the man by the arm and rubbed the studs between his thumb and finger. 'I reckon they would scratch you if you weren't careful.' Bill pulled the guy to his feet and marched him out the office door, down the concrete driveway and onto the footpath. The man didn't resist. Bill manoeuvred him in front of Sully and Charlie, then dropped the man's arm and stepped back.

The guy rubbed his face. 'You had him slap me?' His eyes were wide with disbelief.

Sully slammed a low punch into the man's stomach. The guy bent over, expelling a wheezing breath. Sully kicked his legs, and he fell to the ground. Charlie pulled a small revolver from his pocket, leaned in and stuck the gun in the guy's mouth, making shushing sounds as the man tried to speak.

Bill didn't know what to do. His eyes met those of the guy with the gun in his mouth, and he looked away.

'Here is the message from Markus: Pay up. It's a short message but makes the point, don't you think?' Charlie removed the gun and stood back. Sweat had broken out on the man's head and dribbled down his face. Bill could see the imprint his hand had left on the side of the guy's cheek.

'I don't ...' he said in desperation.

Charlie leaned forward again and flourished the gun in front of the man's face. He pulled back the hammer. 'Right out here, on the street, I'll put a bullet in you. It doesn't matter to us. Markus doesn't want your shitty business. He wants his money. You know how much, plus one week.' Charlie stood upright and put the gun in his pocket.

'Fuck,' the guy yelled at the ground.

Bill stood there, awkwardly.

Sully moved to the car nodding at Bill to do the same. 'Get in'. They drove away in silence until Sully smiled and said to Charlie, 'See? I told you.'

Charlie turned and glanced at Bill, 'Fuck me,' he said. 'Yes, you were right.' He handed Sully a fifty-dollar note. 'Are you busy today, Bill? We have another call to make.'

Bill's stomach flipped with excitement. Just like that, he had become the muscle, and he liked it.

\*\*\*

Two weeks passed. Bill went out with Sully and Charlie four times for pretty much the same result. Bill had realised the set-up was a pantomime of power. They went in, said what they had to say, the guy would refuse or give some excuse, and they would come out and send Bill in. He had slapped two of the guys like he did the first. The other two guys just walked out when he asked them to. Sully and Charlie always asked when they were all back in the car if he had to lay a hand on the guy. It was some sort of check for them. They would nod as if they expected it or raise their eyebrows and glance at each other as if they were surprised.

Bill didn't care though. By then he had had two months of free rent; that is what they had agreed. The more work he did with them, the less rent he had to pay. It staved off a burden and made his welfare payment go a lot further. It was work, he guessed. Not work he wanted, but it seemed to be working for Sully and Charlie. Sully kept smiling every time they got back in the car after visiting some poor guy who needed to pay his debts. There was something satisfying in getting out and doing something, getting the job done. And if pressed, Bill would have to admit he liked the company and being part of a team again.

When they dropped Bill back at his building, Sully would say, 'Good work today, Bill. See you soon.' Charlie would remain silent, but nod and give a polite smile.

\*\*\*

Things changed for Bill one day when, instead of visiting the low end of town, they went to the shiny end, where all the cars were new and houses had electric gates. Bill hadn't seen houses like this in real life. He had grown up in a neighbourhood similar to where he lived now. As they drove along the immaculate blacktopped road, he admired the green, lush lawns in front of high fences topped with hedges and CCTV cameras.

Sully and Charlie sat silently in the front of the big car, not showing any signs of the awe that Bill was feeling. They sat patiently, watching, working, their suits clean and cut square. From where he sat, he could see Sully's square jaw, shaved and smooth. A dimple appeared and disappeared as he clenched and unclenched his teeth. His dark hair was combed back and smooth. Everything about the guy was smooth.

Bill looked down at his large, meaty hands attached to round, red forearms. Bill didn't have many clothes. He usually wore a grey collared t-shirt that he had owned for so long he couldn't remember where he'd got it. It was the same with his black trousers. Had he bought them? Were they issued to him after he'd woken from one of his many drunk-tank visits? The clothes he had on tonight were new, purchased with the money he had saved on rent. He stroked his face. Gritty stubble poked through flabby skin. He had never been a good-looking man; he knew that. His bulbous nose and light-brown flat hair had never given him an edge. He knew where he was in the pecking order of life. Some people naturally knew how the table worked. Some were at the top, with looks, money and personality. And from that point, a sliding scale existed. Some people weren't attractive, but they had personalities that won people over. Some were intelligent and had a purpose. Others were beautiful but horrible people. There were a thousand variants that placed people at different levels on the curve. Bill had always understood where he was on that curve. What he had was the best he was ever going to get.

Although, he didn't think he would ever be this low on the scale if he was honest with himself. And since he had stopped drinking, he had moved a little higher. Not much, but a little. The problem with not drinking was, he was aware of his life position. When he was drunk, well, ignorance was bliss.

Bill had figured out that Charlie understood this too. That is why he only ever gave a nod to Bill. Charlie was too far up the curve to really acknowledge Bill. And that was fine. There seemed to be some sort of sincerity to the way they treated each other. Whatever Charlie asked Bill to do, Bill would do it. It was the natural flow of the curve.

Sully wasn't as high on the scale as Charlie. Sully wasn't as smart but had personality. Sully was further down the line, closer to Bill but not as low as Bill. That is why Sully was nicer to Bill and why Sully understood Bill better. But Sully wouldn't even consider this type of concept. He lived with a different methodology, a different set-up for his life.

Bill had spent forty years as a dock-worker. Forty years with who he thought were his friends, his mates. He saw those men every day; they worked together, shared their lives together and drank together. He thought they were his family. And he thought that was where he belonged in life. He drank and fought side by side with those guys, then he'd walk into the morning sunlight after twelve hours of drinking – backslaps and playful rough hugs before the group separated. Their shift would start with teasing about antics from the drinking sessions. Drunken confessions and dreams all shared with one another.

And then the retrenchments started. The company started to lay off workers and move others into jobs of those who were gone. The unions tried to stop it – brothers marching together to stop the appalling treatment of members. Nothing could halt what the economy had started. The money was gone. The ships weren't coming. Politicians and CEOs made decisions so far away from Bill's position on the curve that he had not even seen it coming. Then the closure came. No more pay cheques. No more work. No more after-work drinking sessions. They all left. His brothers. His colleagues. His friends. Gone. No one called for him. No one checked to see how he was. He chased up a few guys and had a few beers in the first year. After that they disappeared. They had left him. He could see it in their eyes as they had a few awkward quiet beers that he was being left behind. Even those guys were higher up on the curve than Bill.

He stared at the back of Charlie's head. The difference with Charlie was that Charlie knew where he was too. He wasn't at the top of the curve. He was certainly higher than Bill, but Charlie was at peace because he knew he had reached his place. Charlie was where Charlie was supposed to be. And he would be answering to anyone higher than him. This gave Charlie peace to go about his business. There was no secret agenda for him.

And that was life. Lunch was a shit sandwich with a cup of piss to wash it down before you got your teeth kicked in.

Sully spoke, interrupting Bill's thoughts. 'Here it is.'

## 3.

The house was the same as the others on the street. It was a large, modern concrete square with black lights giving it a glow of warmth. A curving driveway cut across perfect green lawns like a river through a hillside landscape. A few manicured trees popped out of the ground as if built rather than grown. What Bill had thought was a three-storey structure was actually only two. The house sat on a raised plateau giving it a castle-like appearance.

The big car turned a concreted loop and eased to a stop just shy of the front door. As usual, Bill waited for direction from the two men in the front seat before making any moves.

Charlie and Sully both popped their doors open. Bill did the same and got out, feeling his new trousers and belt stretch across his lower back. He wasn't up there with Charlie and Sully yet, but he thought he looked pretty good. Buying clothes was something he had not done in a long, long time. A pair of trousers, two collared shirts and a pair of black boots had him feeling good and his new position of whatever it was he was doing had lifted his spirits. He liked doing this work, and he liked having his rent paid. He wanted to keep this job.

They gathered as always at the front of the car for Charlie to give a little pep talk. 'Okay, we know this guy; he is mouthy and has money. He thinks he is on a one-to-one basis with Markus. He is not. Markus has made that clear. This guy is like the rest of them. He owes money. I don't know the layout of the house, so we won't go past the foyer inside. Any questions?'

Bill never had any questions.

Sully asked, 'How do we address this guy?'

Charlie nodded and said, 'His name is Hatchett. We call him Mr Hatchett.'

Sully asked, 'What if someone else is home?'

'There isn't,' Charlie said.

Sully nodded, and Bill caught on. Another of Markus' men must have been watching the house.

They walked to the door and Sully pressed the doorbell button. After a moment, a smiling man opened it, but the smile soon fell when he recognised Charlie and Sully. He was older, around fifty, with receding hair and tanned skin. He wore a white jumper over a blue collared shirt and cargo pants, his feet encased in boat shoes. He looked expensive and like he rated himself highly. 'Gentlemen,' he said and peered down the driveway, searching the street.

Bill wondered if he was checking to see if there were any witnesses to his visitors.

The man backed inside, opening the door wide. 'Come in, come in.'

They filed through into a white-tiled foyer with a carpeted staircase leading to the second level. It was a big space. A white table sat to the side with a large vase that contained dried flower stems set artfully. 'If you would like to join me in the sitting room...' When no one moved, he returned to the foyer, brow furrowing with confusion for a moment before smiling politely.

Sully had positioned himself on the opposite side of the foyer from Charlie. Bill had learned this tactic earlier. It allowed them to watch the target from different angles and to prevent ambushes. Bill stayed near the door to provide another angle of observation and block any attempt to exit.

Charlie said, 'We are here on Markus' behalf.'

The man kept the smile alive, like a performer spinning a plate on a stick. 'Oh, I am sure Markus could just call me if he needed something. Please, come through, I have some beer in the fridge.'

Charlie spoke again. 'Mr Hatchett, Markus has sent us here because he does not wish to speak to you on the phone. We are here to say your time is up. You need to pay what he is owed.'

The smile fell and shattered. 'I beg your pardon. I don't deal with the likes of you. I speak with Markus. I always have, and I always will.'

'Mr Hatchett, with respect, Markus has had a number of phone calls with you. You have missed your deadlines for three months. It is time to face the fact that you need to produce what you owe.'

Hatchett's face turned red. 'How dare you enter my house and speak to me like that. If Markus wants me to do something, he just needs to call. I will not deal with you thugs.' He eyed them individually, lingering on Bill the longest. 'Now, go away, and tell Markus to phone me. Off you trot,' he said with a wave of his hand.

Without thinking, Bill turned to go. The other two folded their arms and stared at Hatchett. When Bill realised the other two weren't moving, he returned to where he'd been standing.

'Are you fucking deaf?' Hatchett yelled at Charlie and Sully. 'The big fucking ox got the idea.' He pointed to the door. 'Fuck off.'

Silence filled the foyer. This time Bill didn't move either.

'Is this supposed to scare me? Are you intimidating me?' Hatchett stomped over to Charlie. 'I will have your nuts as a desk ornament,' he said. He pointed to Sully and then to Bill. 'All your nuts on my desk, hanging from strings and knocking together – knock, knock, knock.'

'Mr Hatchett—' Charlie started.

'Get out of my fucking house. Get out,' he yelled directly at Charlie. 'Take the pretty boy and the fucking elephant and leave my house.'

'Elephant?' Bill whispered.

Hatchet must have heard Bill's words because he returned his attention to him. 'Yes, an elephant in my house. A large, dumb, ugly fucking elephant. Are you here to scare me? With your bulbous nose and your big head? Because it worked. You scare the fuck out of me. You are what I dreamt of as a child – the monster coming to get me. The ogre waiting outside. The beast that will eat me up. What is your purpose here?' Hatchett looked around at the other two men before refocusing on Bill. 'You are a low-life piece of shit and have no business in this house,' he yelled. 'In *my* house!'

Bill stood there, blinking and speechless as he observed Hatchett's red, sweaty face. He wasn't sure what to do. Sully had turned to gaze down the corridor, while Charlie stared at the floor, hands in his pockets. Bill was on his own.

Bill considered his place here. He didn't need to be told he was the lowest in the room. He didn't need to be yelled at.  They were in this man's house because *he* hadn't paid his debts. This guy was no better than Bill. He wasn't 'above' him. He was a pretender and a bully. And Bill's employer didn't like him. Now, it was Bill's turn.

It wasn't a plan ... more a feeling, and Bill rolled with it. He stepped towards Hatchett, hand extended. 'Hi,' he said, 'I'm Bill.'

Probably out of habit, Hatchett accepted Bill's hand which was twice the size of his. But then he sneered. 'Are you fucking kidding, Bill? Get the fuck out of my house!'

Bill looked deep into Hatchett's eyes and squeezed his hand tight. 'Mr Hatchett, with respect, you need to pay Markus.'

Hatchett laughed, but it was shaky. 'I will speak to Markus only,' he said.

Bill squeezed tighter. 'Mr Hatchett, you need to pay Markus.'

The angry expression on Hatchett's face changed to a wince. 'I said I will speak to Markus.'

Bill squeezed tighter again. Hatchett squealed. 'Fuck. You're hurting me.'

The bones under Hatchett's skin jumbled around like a bag of marbles as Bill squeezed even tighter. 'You need to pay Markus.'

Hatchet screamed with pain, his legs gave out and he fell, but Bill held him up by the hand. Bill imagined the bones breaking and tendons snapping as he applied more pressure.

Hatchett found his feet and bounced up, hitting Bill as hard as he could with his other hand. To Bill, it felt like tennis balls bouncing off his body. Hatchett lowered his head and bit the back of Bill's hand. Bill slapped his head away with his left hand, and Hatchett dropped again, crying and screaming, clawing with his free hand, trying to release the trapped one.

Bill leaned down and crushed the hand some more before finally releasing the distraught man.

Hatchett fell to the floor crying and holding the mess that was his right hand. 'Oh fuck, oh fuck,' he said.

Bill stepped back.

Charlie nodded at him and walked to the door. 'Come on, let's go.' Sully followed, keeping an eye on Hatchett. Bill waited a moment, then turned and followed Sully. His stomach lurched. Had he just lost his free rent? Made enemies out of these guys who he was starting to like? It was over. He'd fucked it up.

Sully kept glancing back at the door. 'Get in the car, Bill, but keep your eyes on the garden.' Bill guessed he was checking to see if Hatchet was following them outside with some sort of retribution in mind.

Back in the car, Bill was expecting a lecture, some sort of blow back, Charlie scolding him for over-stepping. But they drove away in silence.

When they reached the highway, Charlie squirmed in the front seat, tucking his gun back in his pants. Bill hadn't realised that Charlie had been carrying a gun. He stared at his hands as they rested on his lap, thinking about the feeling of Hatchett's hand in his. He squeezed his thighs, feeling the power as he peered out the window, watching the buildings grow higher as they got closer to the city heart. His big hands and lack of control may have just lost him this new gig. He knew Charlie and Sully weren't his friends, but he enjoyed their company. He liked being out of his neighbourhood and seeing the world again. He liked having a purpose. But he'd been called an elephant and had crushed a wealthy man's hand. Was that professional behaviour? It couldn't have a good outcome. But that was how it was for guys like Bill. You were down, then you were up, and then you were down.

Bill raised his head to find Sully watching him in the mirror. Their eyes held. Sully was looking at him like he was a zoo animal. Bill broke eye contact first. *Maybe tonight will be the night,* he thought. Maybe, when they dropped him off, he would go out to the dock and dive in. He'd had his little holiday from his life. The meaning of his existence had changed for a short time, but now he realised he couldn't operate in society like a regular person.

Bill was broken and it was time for him to go out of business like all the companies along the docks. Who knows, maybe Charlie and Sully would do it for him. Hatchett was a player, so he had some power and influence around this town. Bill wondered if he'd just crossed a line and would be dealt with accordingly.

'Where are we going?' Bill asked.

Sully was still looking at him. 'We're taking you home.'

*Sounds ominous*, Bill thought. But he was calm; it was coming soon anyway. He just hoped they didn't leave him out for street kids to find him. Kids shouldn't be finding dead bodies.

They rounded the corner that led to his apartment building and stopped at the front door. Bill sat there for a moment, waiting for some instruction, waiting for a gun to appear from the front seats. Nothing happened.

'Are you getting out or what?' Sully said.

So they would put a bullet in him as he walked up the stairs. Fair enough too; no mess in the nice new car. Bill popped the door and got out. He hurried to the stairs, grabbed the railing and placed one foot on the first step. If it was coming, it was coming at that moment.

'Hey, Bill!' It was Charlie's voice. Bill turned around to see Charlie leaning over to speak through the window. 'Good work tonight.'

'Yeah, good work, you big dumb elephant,' Sully said, and they drove off with a roar of the engine, Sully's laugh echoing behind them.

Bill stood on the steps watching the taillights. Good work? He collapsed onto the steps. *Good work*? Charlie had said he'd done good work. He had nowhere to be, so he remained on the step, contemplating what had just happened and how he'd been treated. Sully had been taking the piss, teasing him about being called an elephant, but he'd made the insult funny. By Bill's standards that made Sully his workmate ... a colleague. Bill stroked his cheeks, wondering why they were sore. Then he realised he was smiling; something else that hadn't happened for a very long time.

His thoughts turned to Charlie, the more serious of the two men – older, wiser. It was the first time Charlie had said anything directly to him. What had changed? When Charlie had said 'good work', he was talking about Bill, about the fact that he had stuck up for himself. Another emotion swept through Bill that he hadn't felt for decades – gratitude. He appreciated that Charlie had recognised Bill. As strange as it was, it dawned on Bill that he wasn't alone anymore. Tears suddenly welled in his eyes. He wiped them away quickly.

Returning from his reverie, Bill stood up, the feeling of a numb bum reminding him of the pylon down at the wharf. He looked up at the sky and made out three stars through the city lights. He breathed in deep, filling up his lungs and then emptying them in a big sigh, twice. He hadn't thought of that pylon for weeks or the reason he used to go there.

He went inside to find the building manager standing in the foyer, one hand on her hip, the other holding a cigarette. She scowled at Bill as he walked to the staircase, wiping more tears from his eyes.

'Fucking weirdo,' she muttered as Bill started the climb to his room.

## 4.

The big car rolled up and Sully got out. Charlie remained seated inside. 'Hey,' Sully said looking away.

'Hey,' Bill said, noticing a change in Sully, 'What's happening?'

Sully glanced through the car window at Charlie.

'Tell him,' Charlie said.

Sully turned to face Bill and cleared his throat. 'You are being loaned out.'

'Loaned out? What does that mean?'

Sully put his hands in his pockets. 'We don't like it, Bill. But this has come from the top, from Markus himself. A man will show up soon, and you're to go with him.'

Bill didn't like it either. 'And do what? Who is he?'

'He is us, Bill. He is what Charlie and I are, but for a different organisation.'

As he spoke, a white Mercedes Benz sedan cruised around the corner. They both watched it approach.

'Look,' said Sully, 'Just do what you do for us. We'll see you next week.'

The white car stopped behind Charlie's car. The door opened and an older man with a large moustache stepped out, closed the door and straightened his suit. He scanned the surrounds, then adopted a smile so false he could have tied it to his face. 'You must be Charlie,' he said in an over-friendly tone to Sully.

'I'm Charlie,' Charlie said as he got out of the car. 'You must be Ben.'

The two men walked stiffly towards each other. They were awkward as they shook hands, both smiling, but keeping their distance. Charlie said, 'And this is Sully.' He waved a hand at Sully who nodded in response. Ben nodded to Sully. Neither attempted to shake hands.

'And this is Bill.' Charlie waved towards Bill. 'He's riding with you today.'

Ben placed his hands behind his back and stepped forward in a non-threatening gesture. He looked Bill over. 'Nice to meet you, Bill.' Ben extended a hand, and Bill shook it gently. 'Yes,' Ben said, 'You will do just fine.'

Charlie shook his head ever so slightly at Bill. It was a warning. Charlie wasn't happy about this arrangement either.

'Come on then; let's get going,' Ben said before turning to Charlie. 'You have a nice part of town here.' He opened the driver's door and got in.

Sully grabbed Bill's shoulder and said softly, 'Just do what you do for us. Just get it done and come home.'

'And be respectful; stay out of trouble.' Charlie pressed a wad of cash into his hand. 'For expenses. Don't let them buy you anything.' Bill noticed he said 'them', not Ben. 'You pay your own way for everything.'

Bill nodded. He wasn't sure what the fuss was about. He would go with Ben and do what he did. Free rent is free rent; no matter who was providing it. As he headed to the car, he checked the cash – four fifties. What were 'they' going to buy him for two hundred dollars? Either way, it was a lot of money to have in his pocket that wasn't there when he'd got up that morning.

As Ben drove through the local streets, he occasionally glanced at Bill but neither spoke. The silence wasn't awkward; it was professional. Both men had a job to do and chit chat wasn't part of it. Bill felt a flicker of concern because Charlie and Sully were concerned. He had never seen them worried. He felt like a school kid on his first outing alone.

Forty-five minutes later, Ben manoeuvred the big car through alleyways and past bins to come to a stop behind a group of shops. 'Okay, let's pay old "Tony the Trigger" a visit.'

Bill followed Ben along the lane, past two more shops and into a rear courtyard. A set of yellowing concrete steps led up to an office over the back door of a shop. A cluster of old bins and cardboard boxes, a metropolis for flies and cockroaches, littered the area. He climbed the stairs, wondering what sort of shop it was.

They arrived at a landing with a dark, heavy-looking door. Fortified maybe? Ben raised a fist to knock but stopped and said to Bill, 'This guy calls himself "Tony the Trigger".'

Bill nodded. 'I got it the first time. He has a gun.'

Ben smiled. 'Yeah, maybe.' He knocked on the door.

'What do you want?' a deep voice with a slight accent that Bill couldn't place called out.

'Tony, it's Ben. Let me in. We have to talk.'

There was a sound of scraping chairs and footfalls of people bustling around. The doorknob rattled and a lock was disengaged. The door opened to a small room that smelled of cigars and sweat. Normally a terrible smell, but it was one Bill could relate to. He stepped inside first onto an old, stained carpet with a brown, mottled pattern.

Tony the Trigger was a small man, stereotypically Italian with a gold chain and dark chest hair poking out of a silk shirt that was unbuttoned to the belly. Fat fingers covered in gold rings clasped a stout cigar. He didn't move a muscle as Bill entered but, when he saw Ben, he smiled and stuck his cigar in the side of his mouth. 'Come in, come in, Ben. But I have nothing to fucking tell you.'

'Tony, that's not what I want to hear,' Ben said as he moved in front of Bill. 'We spoke about this. It is time, my friend.'

Tony positioned himself behind a desk covered in papers and files. Behind him, a whiteboard with names and numbers – some circled, some crossed out, and some with arrows pointing from one name to another – was stuck to the wall. Bill couldn't work out what the business was exactly. There was junk everywhere – lots of paper and filing cabinets. The room was hot, ugly and over-lit by ancient fat fluorescent tubes.

Tony pointed his cigar at Bill. 'Who's your new friend? You know, Ben, you don't need to bring new friends around here. *We* are friends Ben. We don't need new fucking friends.'

'This is Bill.'

Tony laughed. 'Bill and Ben? Are you flowerpot men? You don't *need* new friends, Ben. I have all the friends you need.'

'Apparently not,' said Ben dryly, not returning the mirth. 'I'm here to talk to you about our other friends … who you owe a great deal of money to.'

Tony laughed again but shot an uneasy glance at Bill. They spoke for a few minutes in this manner, talking-without-saying-anything banter. He knew to wait. Timing was crucial. Once the banter stopped, it would be time for Bill to act.

He guessed Tony was some sort of loan shark, which wasn't surprising, but something was bugging Bill. He didn't feel comfortable in this room. The mess and the cigar smoke were making him ill ... no ... nervous. He moved to the other side of the room, taking it in from a different angle. The filing cabinets and stacked logbooks formed mountains and valleys through the mist of cigar smoke. It had a picturesque quality, like morning appearing over a mountainside. Adding to the uncomfortable feeling, Tony kept eyeing him while Ben was speaking.

Ben was reading out a list of dates and missed payments. Bill frowned. By now, Tony should be nervous, but he was relaxed as he puffed on his cigar, smiling, seemingly not worried at all. Why was he acting so confident? The money was owed, and the date for repayment had passed. Ben was here to collect one way or another. Maybe it was different on Ben's turf. Maybe the fear that Charlie and Sully induced in people wasn't how it worked here.

Ben was confident too, though, as he told Tony how things were. He wasn't backing down. But a nagging feeling in his gut told Bill something wasn't right.

He returned to stand just behind Ben, who looked over his shoulder, eyebrows furrowed as thought questioning Bill's actions.

Bill returned the frown, and Ben's brows raised in question, but he stayed quiet, letting Bill work.

Tony said, 'Ben, what is it with this guy? He's making me nervous. Get him to move back a little, eh?'

Bill took one step back and surveyed the room. For forty years Bill had moved containers on and off ships – big rectangles that fit together with straight edges – Bill knew what square looked like. This room wasn't square. Something was off. The dimensions were wrong somehow.

Tony reached forward, his eyes on Bill, blowing smoke and knocking ash into an ashtray half-hidden under the mess on his desk. A second cigar was burning in the ashtray. Bill's ill feeling began to manifest into an idea. There was too much smoke in the room for just one cigar. The soggy end of the second cigar pointed outwards, away from Tony and towards Ben. Someone else had been sitting on that chair before Ben. The surprise visit hadn't given them enough time to clean up. So where was that person now?

Charlie and Sully hadn't trained Bill as such, but they had given him tips and they functioned as a team. Charlie had said to Bill, 'If you feel it's off, you let me know.' Bill had never really understood what Charlie had meant until that moment. If Charlie had been there, Bill would say something.

The other two men stared at Bill as he scanned the solid wall behind him that was lined with old, packed shelves between brown filing cabinets. The side walls contained dirty windows that could be mistaken for the walls, except for the dim glow of daylight pushing into the gloom. Bill moved around Ben who watched his movements, eyes alight with interest.

From the different angle, Bill spied it. There was a gap between the walls with a corridor between two filing cabinets. There was another room!

Tony's chair crashed backwards as he sprang to his feet. He opened his mouth to speak just as Bill charged down the corridor. He arrived in a kitchenette with a bathroom opposite, where a small, stout man, chest hair exposed, stood holding a double-barrel shotgun.

The man tried to level the weapon, but Bill grabbed the barrels and forced them upwards. One barrel boomed next to Bill's head, blasting a hole in the roof. Sunshine speared through the smoke and dust to make a star shape on the tiled bathroom floor. Bill reefed the gun upwards out of the man's grip. The man yelped before Bill brought the stock back down into the man's face. His nose snapped, spraying the sunshine star with blood.

Bill yanked the man back to his feet, frisked him and pushed him down the corridor. He pushed him so hard through the filing cabinets that he fell to the floor.

Ben was standing over Tony, pointing a chrome pistol at Tony's chest. 'Tony,' he said, 'Was that for me? Who is this?'

Tony was also on his feet. His confidence had waned substantially. He wasn't smoking now. His hands remained by his side, cigar smoke running up his arm. 'My brother, Angelo,' he mumbled.

'I don't know Angelo. Where are you from, Angelo?' Ben asked.

'Angelo is from my home, Sicily. He is here to stay awhile.'

Ben nodded, dropped the gun from Tony's chest and tapped the gun on his leg as he thought. 'Okay Tony, I see we are at the end of this contract. You just cost yourself a triple penalty, due by Friday. If I don't see the total by Friday, you don't see Saturday. Is that clear?'

'Sure, yes, of course, Ben. Yes, of course.'

Angelo spat blood on the carpet, '*Fanculo*,' he said.

Ben indicated to Bill that it was time to leave. Bill backed up and opened the door. Ben joined him there. 'You bring that money to me, Tony. I am not coming back to this shit hole.' He stepped outside as Angelo groaned and spat more blood. Bill cracked open the shotgun and tipped the shells out. He dropped the empty one to the floor and pocketed the other one, then threw the gun to the far side of the room before walking out.

They trotted down the stairs and hurried to the car. Before they drove off Ben turned Bill. 'Thank you, Bill. Well done.'

ill nodded and stuck his finger in his ear. 'I think I'm deaf.' He hadn't meant it as a joke, but Ben laughed heartily.

## 5.

The weeks that followed were much the same. Charlie and Sully would meet Bill and loan him to other organisations. But their conversations were getting shorter and shorter each time, and Bill was reminded of his lonely past. From the expression on their faces, Charlie and Sully weren't in favour of the situation either.

One Thursday afternoon, Bill had been dropped back at his building after helping out on a job, to find Agatha, the building manager, standing on the front steps. She was standing in her accustomed pose – cigarette burning from an upturned hand, her other hand on her hip. She looked like an old, wrinkly teapot with steam emanating from the spout. Bill didn't want a cup of that.

He strode past her saying, 'Hi,' as he went by.

'They're fucking you.'

Bill stopped and turned back. 'What?'

She pivoted without changing her pose. 'They are fucking you over.'

'Who is?' asked Bill.

She nodded out to the street, to the world. He rolled his eyes as he walked past her.

Agatha called out, 'I know when someone is getting pimped out. Believe me, I know. Been there done that.'

Bill stopped and turned back to her. 'Yeah, I get free rent,' he said.

'You're getting ripped off is what you are.'

She seemed to be challenging him, her eyes unblinking. Bill didn't like that and stepped down to her step. 'What are you talking about?' he said.

'If you would like me to, I could find out a few things. See how much you should be getting.' She sucked on her cigarette, her wrinkled and grossly overpainted lips smacking together like the middle on an accordion. The ash drooped as embers lit up and crackled.

Bill was on the defensive. He worked with gangsters now; he didn't need to take shit from an old slag like her. 'To find out what?' he asked, his tone a little aggressive now.

'Okay, I'll do it,' Agatha said. 'I'll get back to you.' She stomped up the stairs.

'Do what?' Bill said to the sound of the office door slamming shut.

He marched up the stairs thinking that he might take a walk to the pylon tomorrow and refocus. For the first few months after he had teamed up with

Charlie and Sully, he hadn't needed to go there because he'd felt valued, an important team member. But in the past two weeks he'd been out there four times. He wasn't contemplating ending his life like before, but staring at the water relieved the pressure in his head. He found it relaxing.

\*\*\*

Four days later, Bill was wearing a new suit, waiting on the curb for Charlie and Sully. He hoped they wouldn't be too long as he didn't want to bump into Agatha, the crazy old bat. He was glad when he saw the guys come around the corner but wondered who he would be sent off with today.

Sully stopped the car. Charlie lowered his window and said, 'Get in; you're with us today.'

Bill grinned. He got into the back of the car and settled into the comfortable leather seat. 'Hello Charlie, Hello Sully,' he said, still grinning.

Sully turned around in his seat and smiled back. 'Have a look at this bloke; happy as bananas.'

'Not if you turn that banana the other way,' Bill said.

Sully chuckled and turned back to the front. He drove off still smiling.

Charlie spoke from the front passenger seat. 'You've been busy, Bill.'

'No, not really, no more than normal. I just prefer to work with you guys more than the other guys.' Bill was sitting behind Charlie and couldn't see his face. What was he talking about?

'No, I mean you've been busy making phone calls.'

His joy subsided. 'What do you mean? I haven't been speaking to anyone.'

'Are you sure? Someone has been speaking for you, perhaps?'

Bill's stomach sank. 'Where are we going?' he asked, suddenly worried.

'Don't worry, Bill, you're okay. We're going for a coffee and to have a chat.'

A fucking coffee? What the hell was going on? He hadn't done anything that would upset Charlie as far as he knew. He had done what he was told, what he'd been asked to do.

They stopped at a busy corner. Charlie and Sully led Bill into a small coffee shop where a few customers sipped their coffees while reading newspapers or their phones. He slowed his pace, expecting Charlie to pick a table, but Charlie kept walking. Sully followed without breaking stride, so Bill rejoined their line. They marched through the kitchen and out the back door into a car park.

Still in single file, they walked across the car park, across the back lane and through a narrow gate. A footpath took them up to a screen door which Charlie opened without knocking and walked in. Bill followed Sully into another kitchen. This one was bigger and better. Four men in white shirts and caps were chopping up vegetables and other food. None of them looked up. No one acknowledged their presence as they entered a dining area with dark, plush carpet that cushioned Bill's feet. Charlie led them past pristine white tables with black chairs, until they reached a corner table at the back of the room. A man in a suit and tie was sorting invoices and paperwork into neat piles. A calculator sat to one side.

Charlie stopped in front of the table, while Sully walked past him to stand two tables away, facing the front door of the restaurant, his back to Bill and the man in the suit. A defensive position.

The man looked up at Charlie, nodded and said, 'Take a seat just there,' he pointed to the table next to his. Charlie pulled out a chair and sat down. 'Bill,' the man said, 'come here.' The man pointed to the seat across from his.

Bill looked at Charlie, seeking advice. Charlie's facial expression remained blank, but he nodded. Bill sat down.

The man's hair was brown and thin on top. Bill guessed he was probably in his fifties. A thin gold chain hung low over a collared shirt. He wore glasses with thin gold frames and a large moustache covered his top lip – a throwback to the seventies, but he made it work. He had tiny eyes and a head that seemed too big for his body. He gave off a crazy vibe, like anything could trigger him into action. Bill noticed a faint scar that ran down his cheek from just under his eye to the corner of his mouth. 'Pay the Bill, huh?' the man said with a chuckle.

Bill blinked but remained silent, frozen to his chair.

'Relax, Bill. You're okay here. My name is Markus. You've been working for me.'

This was Markus. Bill did relax; he sat back in his seat and nodded.

'Do you talk?' Markus asked.

'Yes, sir, I do. I'm sorry, I didn't know what we were doing here.'

'Hey, don't apologise. Do you want a coffee? Sully, go tell Reggio we need three coffees.' Sully nodded and walked to the kitchen. 'Okay, Bill, you've been doing a great job. You know what's funny? I thought it was these two clowns who were doing the good work.' He pointed to Charlie, who smiled and nodded. 'But then they go on to tell me that they've outsourced their recovery detail! Ha.' He snorted and pointed to Charlie again. 'Who the fuck does that?' Markus laughed. 'These two blood clots, that's who. But anyway, Charlie comes to me and says he has this guy working for him. I say to Charlie, "You don't hire people, Charlie; that's not your fucking job." Charlie says, "Yeah I know, but he's a good guy".'

Sully returned with the coffees at that point, and Markus waved him over to sit with Charlie. 'Sit, Sully. Pay attention and learn something.'

The scent of quality coffee rose up and tantalised Bill's senses. His head spun from the shock of meeting Markus – and wondering why – along with the tantalising aroma of the best coffee he had ever smelt. He wanted to pick up the cup and take a good sniff. But he didn't know what the protocol was. If he had learned anything new in the past few months, it was wait until you're told.

Markus continued. 'What was I saying? Oh yeah, bloody clots. These two guys took it upon themselves to get help with their tasks. That help was you. I called on them one day. I was suspicious, you see; all of a sudden all my risk is coming back to me. The money is returning. I'm saying, "What the fuck is going on?" So I call Charlie. Charlie says, "They're paying the Bill." I don't know what the fuck he is talking about, and he tells me this fucking fairy tale about some down and out, who is the size of a truck, who has been helping them. What was the word you used, Charlie?'

'Assisting,' Charlie said.

'Yeah, assisting. "And the debts are coming good, thanks to Bill." You're Bill. They are paying the Bill. Oh, fuck me, I laughed and laughed, didn't I, Charlie? I laughed and said, "Bullshit. Get rid of him. He hasn't been vetted, and I don't know who the fuck he is".' Markus paused, picked up his cup and took a slurp of coffee.

Bill decided he would do the same.

'Charlie, though,' Markus went on, 'he didn't do what I told him. He decided to keep using you. He told me, "No, I like this guy. He gets the job done without a fuss. He is solid." Charlie said that about you, Bill.'

Bill and Charlie exchanged a look.

Markus continued. 'So I say, "The fuck you doing?" Charlie says, "*He* is the one getting the results. It's Bill who is getting the money." So what can I do? It's all good. Until one day I get a phone call from the Letzio family. They ask if they can borrow you.' Markus' eyes grew wide. 'Yeah, can you believe it? They phone me and ask if they can borrow you. Like you're a fucking lawnmower.'

Bill smiled politely. He brought the cup to his lips and let the scent invade his nostrils. His mouth watered.

Markus went on. 'You start doing your thing for other organisations, and people keep telling me, "Paying the Bill". I hear it everywhere. Everyone is getting all their debts back, and things are rosy. We should have a t-shirt made with Paying the Bill printed on it.'

Suddenly, his face went serious. 'Sully, bring her in.' He turned back to Bill. 'Against my better judgement, but under pressure from these idiots, I am going to take a chance on this.'

Bill heard a noise behind him. He turned to see Sully returning from the kitchen with Agatha closely following. Surprised, Bill choked on his hot coffee. He coughed and liquid splattered the table.

As Sully brought Agatha to a standstill beside Bill, he asked, 'Are you okay, Bill?'

Bill nodded and wiped his mouth.

Sully offered Agatha a chair next to Bill. As she sat, she said to Bill, 'Nice to see you too.'

Markus leant forward. His casual banter had faded and he said sternly, 'Quiet, Agatha. I was about to explain to Bill what's going on.'

Agatha pursed her lips and crossed her legs. He understood she was doing what she was told. Markus was the boss here.

Bill thought Agatha looked tiny among these dangerous men who looked like they could cut your throat without getting a drop of blood on their expensive shoes. And Bill was a giant compared to her petite frame. He could pick her up and throw her across a highway. He wondered how she had become involved with them. Was she there by choice? She had commented on being pimped out. She seemed tough enough to be an old call-girl.

'... Don't you think so, Bill?' Markus said, demanding Bill's attention.

'Uh, sorry, what?'

'For fuck's sake, Bill, listen,' Agatha said to him.

'It doesn't matter,' Markus said. 'Anyway, let's get down to it. You are all here as a business suggestion from Agatha. She proposed that this collection business be formalised – somewhat – and some terms set out.' He paused and took a sip of coffee.

Bill did the same, but the taste seemed to have soured. He needn't have worried about Agatha in the present company. She could hold her own.

Markus continued. 'The proposal is this: Bill will go freelance with Agatha managing the books for him. Agatha has had experience managing other businesses for me in the past. Originally, we thought we'd go with the "buying of debt" model, but after some consideration and a brainwave from Agatha, we're not doing that. Instead, we're going with a flat rate, quoted, before each job.'

Charlie made a noise in his throat.

Markus held up a hand. 'Yeah, I know, but this could work for us, because it keeps us out of other people's businesses. We shall negotiate a fee based on the outstanding debt and risk assessment. This leaves us out of any ongoing disputes. The profits will be fifty-fifty. Fifty per cent to the house, and fifty per cent to cover costs and wages.' Markus pointed to Bill and Agatha.

Before he could stop himself, Bill said, 'What about those guys?' and pointed to Charlie and Sully.

Markus said, 'They work for me, Bill. I pay them. They will oversee the project and can be of assistance to you if needed. They will check in with you and represent me and my interests. If you have any issues, you call them. They will sort it out. Your role is just the collection of debt.'

Agatha smiled at Bill, her brown teeth showing between her overdone red lips. 'We'll be partners, Bill.'

## 6.

Bill didn't understand the nuts and the bolts of the business. In basic terms, Agatha booked Bill's airline tickets, and he flew to a different city each week to be menacing on a national level. Agatha said it was bad business to be in the one city too often. Bill didn't care as he hadn't travelled before. He had never even left the city. He liked visiting new places. He liked going back to a city he had already visited to explore some more.

Sometimes, after Charlie and Sully had dropped him at the airport, Bill would wander around with the small bag on wheels that Agatha had purchased for him. This was the part he enjoyed the most. There was a certain kinship between travellers – a type of fellowship of common goals, to be going somewhere and blame the airlines for any deviations from the plan. Bill found himself sharing a smile with parents as their noisy kids grew restless while waiting. He stood in the group as everyone shook their heads at the time it took for the baggage to come to the carousel. Bill usually didn't have to collect luggage; all he had was his carry-on bag, but he stood in the crowd anyway, enjoying the feeling of belonging to a group.

He wasn't all that jazzed on the actual flying part. The aeroplane seats were somewhat narrow for his large frame, which made his ride uncomfortable. He also saw his fellow passengers' alarmed expressions when they realised they were to be seated next to a giant. And his fingers were too large to eat airline food with any dignity or without elbowing his neighbour when opening a container. He did, however, like the nice rooms in the hotels he stayed in. The clean sheets smelled like perfume, and he liked being called 'Sir' as he went about his life. This new and shiny world of being a contract stand-over man was great.

On each trip, men of various shapes, sizes and colours met him at either the airport or the hotel. He knew their purpose. Whether they were white guys in suits or young guys in track pants, white shirts and multiple gold chains, they were all Charlie and Sully. Bill didn't really like these guys, though. They didn't treat him like Charlie and Sully did. They weren't colleagues or workmates. Bill was simply a hired tool. They would pick him up and take him to various places, like offices, factories and sometimes a person's home. He stood where he was told and waited until someone walked out and gave him 'the look' before going inside. He would ask politely, then with increasing menace, until the money was given up. Sometimes he would need to slap the guy a bit, but usually, it was just Bill standing there that was enough of a threat. The guy didn't know who Bill was and would sometimes try to coerce a different result, offering Bill money or drugs, sometimes women and boys, depending on the nature of the business. Bill would usually slap the guy at this point to send a signal that he wasn't trading loyalties. The message was delivered to the poor grovelling sod who owed someone something. Bill feigned disgust at the victim's desperation to ensure his own position was never questioned by his employers. In truth though, sometimes, Bill felt bad for the guy who was on his knees before him, just trying to survive.

Once his work was done, he was driven back to the hotel or straight back to the airport. Bill enjoyed the travel and the life but, as he got closer to home, the good feelings would leave him. And each time he arrived back in his own city and back to his little bedsit, the shadows would come after him again. As his mood darkened, the pylon would sometimes enter his thoughts.

*** 

The legend of 'Paying the Bill' grew across the country. Rumours circulated from city to city of torture sessions that lasted days and about the obsessed debt collector who had become a psychotic stalker. If there was unaccounted money, Bill would track you down and make you pay. If you didn't, he would knock out an eardrum or fracture your skull with a slap. Stories flew around bars and gambling dens about a man with a crushed hand and how Bill had survived a shotgun blast. Another story told of Bill slapping someone so hard that he dislocated the man's jaw, leaving him with a permanent disability.

As a result, Bill's task became easier. On some occasions, men would break down and cry when they realised who he was. They would reveal the secret safe hidden in the floor or an offshore bank account in their wife's name. As soon as they knew they had to 'Pay the Bill', they arranged to pay the outstanding balance quick smart.

Bill didn't wait around for the money. He did not accept a cent on anyone else's behalf, even when wads of cash were placed at his feet. Charlie had told him not to touch anything of value, literally. 'Keep it simple, Bill; if something of value comes into the mix, just step away.'

Oddly, Agatha had told him the same thing on a different occasion. 'And don't you take a fucking cent. It's not yours; that's what the lackeys are for. You just get out of the way if the money shows up. Get out of the room. Fuck that, Bill. You're there to make them pay, not clean up the mess. Things get fucked up around cash.'

Bill didn't really understand what she was talking about but he did what he was told.

## 7.

Bill stopped at the bottom of the staircase, swinging his wheelie suitcase up two steps in front of him and looked up. The old building he called home loomed above him. Windows were lit in a random pattern giving it a checkerboard effect, the chess pieces scattered though the building. *This would be the view of a fallen chess pawn*, he thought. His shoulders dropped as the darkness in his mood returned.

'Why are you so bummed?'

Startled, Bill narrowed his gaze and saw Agatha standing at the top of the stairs. The single red dot of her cigarette glowed dimly as she spied on him from the shadows. 'I'm not; I'm just looking.' 'Looking?' Agatha said as if it was a strange concept she had never come across. 'Stop *looking* and get up here.'

He was tired and short of patience; it was the third time he'd been away this month. 'I would like to go to bed.'

'Bed? Fuck off!' Agatha said with a laugh. 'Come here. I have to show you something.'

Bill sighed. He wasn't sure what Agatha was talking about. They had spoken little since the restaurant, apart from the odd hello and when Agatha gave him instructions for his next job, like where he was going and what time 'The Boys', as she called Charlie and Sully, would be picking him up. Bill usually nodded and smiled, always ready for a chance to hang out with 'The Boys'. It was all fairly routine. It wasn't like he considered Agatha a friend or anything. She was just Agatha, the crazy building manager who was now managing him.

With reluctance, Bill dragged his suitcase up the stairs and followed her into her office, copping the extended tail of cigarette smoke in his face. He dropped his bag by the door and followed her into a back room. She switched on the light, giving Bill an eyeful of her thin, pink hair and dry scalp as he towered above her.

'Have a fucking look!' she said and waved her hand like a TV game-show host showing off a new car.

But it was more than a new car he saw; it was a room piled with cash. Clear-plastic boxes containing stacks and stacks of money were piled up three high in one corner. She must have run out of boxes because more cash was bundled with rubber bands and stacked on top of each other. It was like a pile of house bricks but made of money. The whole corner of the room was covered in cash.

She looked up at him and smiled. 'You're rich, you are,' she said with pride.

'Bloody hell,' he said, 'How much is there?'

'A fucking lot,' she said. 'Four hundred and sixty-seven thousand, three hundred and fifty-five dollars.'

'You're a clever old moll.'

'I fucking am.'

'Can I have some?'

'I don't see why not; it's yours.'

'What about you? Where's yours?'

'It's there too. Don't worry about that.'

Bill picked up a stack of notes. He bounced the stack in his hand. For the first time in a long time, Bill had a thirst.

## 8.

Bill woke to a crushing feeling in his head. It felt like his mouth had been sealed shut with glue. His eyelids didn't want to part.

He concentrated hard. Carefully and slowly, he managed to separate his lips and open his eyes, the latter coming apart like a pair of zip lock bags. He blinked a couple of times to clear his blurry vision. He was wedged in the corner of an old room, sitting upright. The floor was hardwood and bare. A single timber door sat on an odd angle from the frame to the floor. The lock was broken. Paint peeled from ceiling above him.

He worked his jaw to peel his swollen tongue away from the roof of his mouth, then moved his tongue around to lubricate the inner workings. His mind was foggy and sluggish to start functioning. Beams of sunlight stabbed through a filthy window just above his head and the smells of burnt wood, body odour and something acidic finally rebooted his senses.

A sudden rush of self-awareness hit Bill hard. He sat forward, the movement causing a dull boom as the headache claimed real estate in his skull. He winced. The room was filthy and derelict. Where was he? In an abandoned house? The walls were spray painted with graffiti. A large 'cock and balls' painted in red peered at him like a two-dimensional voyeur watching as he'd slept.

Slowly, Bill started to move. He got to his feet, dizzy and uncertain, leaning one hand on the wall for stability. He hurt all over. Felt sick in the stomach.

A mattress lay on the grubby timber floor, pushed to one corner like a rotten and forgotten corpse. Dark stains created cloud shapes of varying shades of grey and black on its cover. Bill imagined the blood, semen and vomit that must have caused the offensive blemishes.

Pushing off from the wall, Bill exited through the door that led into a larger room. There was no furniture in what he guessed might have been a living room once. Beer bottles littered the floor and a discarded wine cask lay on its side. He leaned against the door frame to map the layout and find a way out. Spying a door at the far end of a hallway, he lurched forward, letting gravity assist his heavy gait.

The pounding in his head increased as he tried to open the door to the outside. The handle turned easily enough, but the door stuck due to a two-litre plastic milk carton filled with tiny orange caps blocking its path. He kicked it aside, the seedy contents of used syringes rattling inside. Where the fuck was he? A crack house?

Sunlight attacked his eyes like an electrical current as he walked outside. The heat of the day pressed down on his neck and shoulders. His entire body rejected the idea of walking … of moving at all. His lungs couldn't seem to get enough air as he passed through the yard onto the roadway. Or was it a lane? No, it was a footpath. He had come out the back door.

He staggered past white picket fences, trimmed shrubbery and tidy houses. It looked like a nice neighbourhood. Why was there a crack house in a nice neighbourhood? He had no idea. He had no idea where he was. Turning left at the next intersection, his foot caught on a crack in the concrete and he stumbled. A dog barked at him through a fence, making him jump. He wrinkled his nose as he regained his balance. *People should clean up after their dogs,* he thought. Then he realised it was his own odour he could smell.

Up ahead, a woman came around the corner pushing a pram. The young mother paused when she saw Bill. Her head darted around, looking for another route, and she spun the pram ninety degrees to quickly cross the road.

Bill's urge to call out to her, say he's not a threat, was mitigated by a chunk of phlegm he coughed up. Shame shot through Bill. He must look terrible. He knew he smelt terrible. He didn't want to scare anyone. Not anymore. Not again. Especially young mothers. He waited until the young mother had gone around the corner before spitting the sputum on a bush.

Bill turned his head towards the sound of heavy traffic. A main road! The sound acts as a beacon, guiding him towards a destination. He searched his pockets but knew he'd come up empty. He had no cash for a cab or a bus. Was he robbed? He had piles of cash at home, but who would believe that in his current state?

He reached the main road with a sense of achievement. The road sign told him it would be a two-hour walk home. He took a deep breath, thinking, *One foot in front of the other*. This journey would be longer than twelve steps.

Two-and-a-half hours later, Bill rounded the final corner before his building. Depression had gripped his mind the whole way home. He knew what was happening to him. He had done this before. Depression came after drinking. The feeling of losing yourself to another power stole your soul for a period of time. It felt like you'd borrowed today, that the time you existed in wasn't yours, and you needed to pay it back. The feeling had grown with each step because the closer he got to home, the more likely he would meet someone in the street. And God forbid if Charlie or Sully were waiting for him. He couldn't work today. Not like this. They would take one look at him and form 'the opinion'. That's what his dock-worker mates used to call it when they got in trouble from their spouses. That look of pity and scorn. They would laugh about it and the lies they told at the next drinking session. Bill had never had a spouse, but he saw the opinion when he used to drink full time. It was the moment when a person realised what he was. And Bill was a drunk ... an alcoholic.

He didn't want to be that anymore. More than ever before, he didn't want to be that.

His feet were hot and ached from the miles they had just put in. He could feel his pant legs gripping his crotch as he picked up the pace to get to his door as soon as he could. He was chafed, hot and smelly. He needed a plan – get up the stairs, through his front door and get in the shower. Wash it off. Wash it all off. Start from there.

Head down, he marched on, ignoring the world that held him in contempt. He stared at the ground as he walked. The cracks and weeds that flagged his route were all familiar. He walked fast, determined to get through the front doors. At the last moment, he looked up and nearly walked into the back of an ambulance. He stopped dead and frowned. There was no one around. Just then, the front doors of the building burst open and two ambulance officers hurried out, lifted a gurney down the front steps and headed towards the ambulance.

One ambulance officer yelled, 'Get out of the way. Move.' He flung the rear doors open, and he and his partner lifted the trolley inside.

Bill saw Agatha's small head poking out from under the sheet. 'That's Agatha,' he said dumbly.

'Yeah, thanks,' said the ambulance officer, slamming the back doors closed behind Agatha and the attending paramedic.

'What happened?' asked Bill. 'I know her.'

'Just get out of the way,' the ambulance driver replied.

'Hey,' Bill said and grabbed the man's arm. 'I know her! What fucking happened?'

Halfway in his seat, the officer said over his shoulder, 'She overdosed. Heart problem. Gotta go.' He disappeared into the cab and slammed the door. The siren screamed as the ambulance drove away. The blue and red light fading with the sound. Bill watched until it was gone.

The street went quiet. He turned and walked up the stairs into the foyer. The office door had been left ajar, presumably by the ambulance officers who had just treated Agatha. The lights were on too. Someone must have found her, called an ambulance for her. He should probably lock the door. Agatha might have personal possessions or even some cash in the desk …

Cash! *Oh my God,* he thought. *The money*!

Bill ran inside. First-aid packets and assorted rubbish lay strewn on the ground. He rushed to the back room where the money was stored. Turned the doorknob. It didn't turn. It was locked. He exhaled with relief. *Clever old moll.*

## 9.

Two days later, Bill sat opposite Agatha in her office. They sat in silence, not sure where to begin. She looked pale and thin. Smaller than before. They looked at each other and then away, to the floor or the ceiling. Anywhere but at each other.

The sun shone through the opaque windows, bathing them both in a spotlight. Bill wanted to tell her what had happened to him. That he had suffered a similar fate, that the temptation the money presented was too great. She was not alone in her suffering. He wanted to offer words of comfort, but he couldn't. Instead they simply sat together. This said as much as words. Their awkward bond was acknowledged.

Without knocking, Sully walked into the room. 'Bill, I've been looking for you. We have a job.' He looked at Agatha and back at Bill. Picked up the vibe. 'Ah, I'll meet you outside in a minute, yeah?'

Bill looked at Agatha and she nodded. This was business; they could talk later. He hastened outside to catch up with Sully.

Charlie and Sully were waiting by the car. Bill said, 'Where am I going this time?'

'Go get your suit on,' Charlie said. 'See you here back here in a minute.'

Inside his apartment, Bill threw on a suit as fast as he could. Minutes later, he was in the back seat of the big car. Back with the boys – where he preferred to be.

Sully started the big engine and pulled out and around the corner. Somehow, this felt ominous to Bill.

'What happened?' Sully asked.

Bill sighed. He needed to tell someone. It may very well be the end of his employment and his time with these guys. 'I spent some money.'

Sully said, 'Oh yeah? What did you buy?'

'A headache.'

Sully smiled ruefully and glanced at Charlie, who gave a faint nod. Sully continued. 'Yeah, we figured as much. We were looking for you. There was a job on and you weren't anywhere to be found. We heard you were out having a good time on the town.'

Bill was surprised. 'You heard?'

'Yeah, once we realised you were not here, we went looking for you. We were worried about you. We were worried someone got you.'

Oddly, this made Bill feel better and worse at the same time. He really did have workmates again. They were different from his old workmates from the docks, but this was a different business. These guys had made the effort to locate him. 'Where was I?'

Sully looked at Charlie again. 'We stopped looking when we heard what you were doing. You were okay; that's all that matters.'

Bill felt even worse. He looked down at his big hands.

Charlie's phone rang and he answered it. 'Yeah, okay. Ah, no not today. Thanks,' he said and put the phone down. Sully put his blinker on and turned the car around.

Charlie peered out the windscreen, into the bright day. 'Bill, money is a tool. It is a method of doing something. And like a tool, it can be dangerous. I don't want to offend you, but I think you need to hear this from us before someone else delivers this message to you differently. So this is *us* talking to *you.*'

Bill said, 'Go on, Charlie. I'm listening.' Charlie wouldn't say anything unless it was worth hearing. Bill knew that much.

'I am not telling you what to do. You do whatever you want. But I think you are out of practice. You've been living in the dark for some time, and through this happenstance with us, you are now back in the light. I know you a little now, and I know Sully feels the same way.'

Sully nodded, his attention on the road ahead.

Bill flushed, embarrassed that these men he admired knew about his weakness.

'Bill, that money...No, *earning* that money the way you do is not the problem. The fact you have it says you earned it fair and square. The problem is what to do with it. You need to reverse the earnings in some way to get what you need. Your life has changed. It's so different to twenty years ago when you were a dock-worker. You need to reverse engineer what that money means to you.'

Charlie turned in his seat and looked Bill in the eye. 'Ask yourself what you need from that money. Don't let your life get away from you now. Not while you're in front. So what can the money do for you? You may have earned it by doing – let's just say – some seedy things, but it's been laundered. Earned dirty but made clean. Now, you can do what you want with it – buy a race car or a boat. Pay for three hookers to take on your boat, if that's what you want. As long as it's *good* for you. But if the money is going to harm you, reverse launder it. Take that money and do some good. Whatever that may be for you.' Charlie turned back to the windscreen.

Feeling like he'd been hit low and hard in the heart, Bill looked out the window and saw they were pulling up outside his apartment block.

'We'll see you in a few days, Bill,' Charlie said.

Bill hopped out, stepping over some rubbish accumulated on the curb.

Sully waved out the window. 'See you next week, Bill. Take it easy.'

Bill turned and saw Agatha standing at the top of the stairs staring at him, eyes creased with worry. He gave her a curt nod as he walked past.

That night for Bill was remarkably the same as every other night except for the turmoil in his mind. He ate and showered while Charlie's words spun around in his thoughts. *Reverse launder the money*. He contemplated his future. Compared it to his past.

*Reverse launder the money.*

Bill fell asleep with these thoughts and slept fitfully. In the morning, as he sat drinking coffee, looking out his tiny window, he recalled a dream from the previous night. He remembered standing on the side of a city road, panicked, trying to move but couldn't. He called out to get the attention of two old men standing in the middle of the street, but they didn't hear. He waved frantically, but the men couldn't see him. He tried to move forward, but there was an unseen barrier. One of the men was clean shaven and well dressed in a dark suit. He was taller than the other man. No, not taller – he stood erect with a straight back. Bill waved and called out. The other man's posture was bent. He had long, greasy hair and an unkempt beard. This man was dressed in track pants and slippers. His shirt was old and jacket, worn and faded. The men didn't talk; they just stood next each other, watching the road as if expecting something to arrive. As much as Bill tried, he couldn't get their attention or reach them. Dread encompassed Bill. They were going to get hurt. He didn't know why, but he needed to get the men off the road.

Rinsing his coffee cup in the tiny sink, he knew what he had to do. While drinking his coffee, Bill realised who the two old men were. Both men standing on the road were two different versions of himself.

## 10.

Bill wore his suit. It felt right.

He and Agatha stood at the entry of the church while they waited for the priest to arrive. A woman who had been arranging flowers had gone off to find him. Big timber doors were folded back allowing a view of rows of wooden pews. The sun's rays, tinted various colours from the stained-glass windows, lit up the interior.

The priest arrived from the outside of the building. For some reason this surprised Bill. The priest was an older man, maybe mid-sixties. He wore black and filled out the shirt with a muscular body. He had some scarring around his eyes and fat ears. Bill recognised the traits of a boxer.

The priest invited them inside and introduced himself as Father O'Conner. As they walked down the aisle, Father O'Conner providing some light banter about the history of the church, Bill noticed how lightly he walked, his footfalls barely making a noise on the timber floor. He had small eyes that pierced you like fishing hooks, trying to land your emotions, capture your soul. His white hair was clipped short. Bill had liked him straightaway. He was the sort of guy who had been down in the muck himself; he didn't just preach about it. This was a guy who listened and had a brain. He had the experience to deal with other people's problems because he'd done a few rounds with his own demons.

They walked through stone arches with hanging lights and passed by the altar with a large crucifix of Jesus impaled and bleeding behind it. 'Once, this church was a mini cathedral that housed the beliefs and concerns of the entire neighbourhood,' the priest explained. 'Now, it caters to the few who remembered what faith was or to those who need to find it for the first time.'

Bill guessed there was a gap in the congregation these days. Modern society was tailored for atheists and those who found solace in chemicals. Not that this was a new issue. Alcohol, drugs, and even sex were once sins requiring redemption. Now, these sins were accepted. The church catered for the true believers and the truly lost. Two ends of the scale. Everything in the middle was business as usual in the big city. No absolution required.

Bill stared at the nails in the hands and feet of Jesus on the crucifix. They reminded him of how Charlie had called money a tool. Bill understood completely. The hammer and the nails were tools used to crucify. Charlie was a smart man.

They left the church through a side door that led to a concreted area with high fences and metal picnic tables. The stone church wall stood tall and strong behind them. A fence set in the same stone ran high along the other side of the courtyard. Agatha looked around and said, 'Looks like a fucking jail,' then remembering her company, 'Oh, sorry, Father.'

The priest laughed it off. 'Unfortunately, the fences are required. And the swearing is necessary to describe them. Don't worry, I've heard worse. I've *said* worse.' He sat at one of the metal picnic tables and asked Agatha and Bill to do the same. He sat straight and placed one hand over the other ready to listen. 'I'm Father Ed O'Conner. Call me Ed.'

Bill nodded and let Agatha do the introductions. 'I'm Agatha, and this is Bill.'

Father Ed nodded, 'Hello Agatha. Hello Bill. You look like you do some work, Bill. Do you box?'

'No,' said Bill. 'Not the way you do.'

Father Ed gave a practised smile, obviously confused by the answer, but Bill let it go.

'So, how can I help you?' Ed asked.

'We have a proposition for you,' Agatha said. 'It may sound odd at first, but please hear us out.'

Ed nodded. 'Okay, I'm game if you are.'

Bill remained silent so, after giving him a dirty look, Agatha forged ahead. 'We have some money. We would like to make a donation to your church.'

Father Ed opened his mouth to say something, but Agatha jumped in before he could. 'We want to sponsor a program. We have a significant amount of money and need to do something with it. It's—'

Ed jumped in, holding both hands up in a stop motion. 'Okay, hang on. We don't do that here. This church is legitimate, and I am accountable for what happens. We do not work with organisations that,' he paused, 'require money to be moved.'

Agatha smiled her own practised smile. 'No, that's not what we mean. We don't want the money back. We want to sponsor a program that you can run – something you may have been wanting to start but haven't had the funds.'

'Look, I think I understand. I appreciate the offer and the sentiment. I don't know who you represent, but you have to understand, this is a church. We look after people here. I can't place any ownership on that. People come here to *be* helped. Other people come here *to* help. One is not more important than the other. It's not a service that is up for sale but a way of life. And it's a neutral place.'

Agatha opened her mouth to speak, but Father Ed carried on before she got a word out.

'I don't expect everyone who walks through those front doors to believe in God or to have faith. And that is the point of this place and the people in it. When those people walk back out of those same doors, hopefully, they have a little bit more of something they lacked when they came in. That is what *I* do. I help restore those who need restoring. And if those people come back, they can contribute to that process a little bit too – maybe contribute to someone else's well-being – by walking out with a healthier soul than when they walked in.'

The speech sounded rehearsed to Bill. The man was a preacher after all. Corruption had tried to breach these walls before and failed. Father Ed saw the warning signs and categorised their offer as an attack.

Agatha crossed her arms and laid out the bare facts in her typical Agatha way. 'Yes, we know what a church is. What we have is money. We want to give it to you.'

'I get it. I do. But we aren't here for that. I can't go down a path of free money.'

'Why not?' asked Agatha.

'Because of what I just said; this place must remain neutral. The church can't help others if it is biased or selective. The doors are open to everyone, all the time. To be honest, I don't even care what religion a person is faithful to. If they need spiritual healing, they can get it here, whoever they are, for the right reasons. And if you guys are from a place that I think you are, you will understand that.'

Agatha sat up straight. 'What is that supposed to mean?'

Ed narrowed his eyes, and Bill recognised the fighter within. He imagined those eyes during a fight – focused, determined – an indication that the defensive tactics were about to get shelved and a knockout punch was coming.

'Agatha,' Bill said, 'you know what he means. And he's right. Ed, I need to explain where the money is coming from. Please, as Agatha said at the beginning, hear me out.'

Father Ed switched his attention back and forth between the two as if expecting an attack from each side. He settled on Bill and raised an eyebrow as though to say, 'Give me your best shot'.

Bill thought for a moment about Charlie's recent advice. Bill was a different person these days, and this is where he took control of his life. Right here, right now, with an ex-boxer priest and an ex-prostitute business manager. It was time for courage. Time to speak up.

He began hesitantly. 'I earn my money by standing over men who have not paid back their debts to, er, the organisations you speak of. I haven't been doing it for very long, and the odd thing is, I'm really good at it. I didn't try to be; I just am. I mean, look at me; half the guys cough up the cash before I even speak. They don't know me, and they don't care who I am. I don't care who they are. But they are all in the game. All they know is that I am there for one of two reasons – to collect the cash or hurt them.'

Bill had expected an interruption, but Father Ed was quiet. His eyes were still narrow and focused though. He was listening. Bill guessed he'd heard many, many stories like this before.

'They say, "Pay the Bill" when they refer to me. Bill … that's me. It's a silly nickname that precedes everything I do for these organisations. It's marketing – a tagline. I get results because half the job is done before I even get there. And we are making money by collecting money. I understand what you're saying, but we can't spend what we make because …' Bill paused looking for the words, 'we do more damage than good.'

Father Ed slapped his hands on the table and stood up. 'I can't help you. You guys need an accountant, not a tax write-off. I will not repeat myself. You are both welcome back here at any time, but please don't bring the money with you. I will not accept it. Goodbye.' He turned away and headed towards the door to the church.

Agatha swore and turned to Bill, who rose to his feet and called after the priest, 'I'm an alcoholic.'

Ed stopped with his hand on the door handle. He turned back towards them, his eyes softer, lighter ... interested.

Bill stood and moved closer to Ed. 'I don't know how to explain it, but I think you've heard this sort of stuff before, so I will just put it out there,' he said. 'I've been collecting bad debts, but I have one of my own – the bill for me, for my life. My debt is that I haven't achieved anything or contributed to anything. I have a debt to settle, and whether it is with God, or society, or to my mother, wherever the fuck she is, I don't know. But I have a debt to settle for my being here on this planet. I need to contribute in some way. And the only way I know how to do that is to do what I do best, and that is debt collection for organised crime. I have no other means or skills. You said the money is not worth anything here because you can't be bought. Well that is exactly why we need to bring the money we earn to you. We don't want to buy anything. I am too old and too tired to start again. We just want to leave something for someone else.'

Bill glanced back at Agatha. She was sitting with her head down, quietly crying and nodding.

'Please, Ed, let us take some of the bad in this city and make it good. It's reverse laundering. I want to even up the score. I want to pay my bill.'

Ed raised his eyes to the sky as if asking for a higher power for advice, before saying, 'And what do you want from this? Do you think you will get into Heaven if you *pay* for your sins?'

Bill flushed, annoyed at his words. He thrust his face at the priest, letting the boxer see the mobster. 'No, Father, I don't. I think my chance for Heaven has come and gone. But I may help someone else get there. That is what I want. That is when my debt is settled.'

# 11.

Bill dressed in his new suit. He didn't struggle with the top button to close the collar around his neck as he usually did. This suit was tailored and, even though he knew he was an odd-looking guy in general, he wanted to look good tonight. He was large and cumbersome – a hippo in a tutu. He knew he would draw looks from other people, but he didn't care. He knew who he was and what he had done. He was the guy at the end of the line, the last resort and the bottom of the pile. That is what he was and always would be. He drew a breath, admiring his crisp white shirt and dark navy suit and tie. He *did* look good.

He *felt* good.

He had done the right thing; that was evident from what he and Agatha had achieved. Even though to achieve that good outcome, he had to be bad. By lying down with dogs, he came up with fleas, and those fleas were worth money. And it was what they did with that money that created a newfound pride in himself.

Tonight, the invitation was for the grand opening of the new youth and community centre. Father Ed had taken their money and, by Bill and Agatha's request, had never informed anyone where the funds had come from. That is what had solidified the deal with Father Ed. It meant that the donations were altruistic, that they came from a good place, and not for financial or personal gain. If pressed, Father Ed would say, 'an anonymous benefactor'. Only churches and charities got away with that.

Charlie and Sully had worked it out. When going about business with Bill, if they happened to drive past the community centre construction site, one of them would say, 'Nice looking building that' or 'That looks expensive; must have a wealthy donor' And they would look at Bill with a twinkle in their eyes.

Bill slipped the invitation into his coat pocket. He had a sudden urge. He checked his watch and saw that he had enough time. He opened the old door to his tiny bedsit and walked quickly down the stairs; he didn't want to bump into any neighbours while he was wearing his suit. Not that he didn't want to show off, but if they suspected he had cash, they would burgle his apartment while he was out.

The cool air hit his face as he walked down the stairs to the road. Instead of turning left towards the church, he turned right towards the old wharf. Being careful not to let his suit make contact with the rusty metal, he pushed the old chain gate apart and stepped through. It had been at least a year since he had taken this walk, and he took deep breaths of salty air. The old pylon that he had sat upon for so long stood still and stoic against a dark and tranquil sea. Water slapped the concrete below in playful gestures as a breeze ran along the decaying wharf making his suit jacket flap. He arrived at the spot where he used to sit and looked at the empty space at the top of the pylon. He stood by his old self and compared the view.

Thrusting his hands in his pockets, he thought about his past – the low days when he had nothing left, nothing to pursue, not even the drink. He realised how he had hollowed out his life. Alcohol had washed the future right out of him, and he hadn't noticed. He'd come so close back then, so close to falling into the water and ending his existence. And there would have been no consequence. He would have been just another hobo putting himself out of his own misery.

But here he was still – alive and well. He had given back and was paying his debt. He might even be ... happy? He stared across the water, looked up to the stars. He was proud of himself. That's what it was. Whether happy or proud, it felt good. He hadn't felt like this for a very long time.

A noise behind him made him turn. In the poor light, all he could see were the edges of old buildings and cranes defined by shades of dark. He turned back to the water, but then again – footsteps, light and on gravel. Bill turned around and saw movement in the darkness, a shadow moving in the shadows. The footsteps came at him. A shape began to emerge. For a moment, Bill couldn't figure out what the shape was. As the shape drew near, the outline became clearer. It was a short man, round in the middle, wearing a hooded jacket which changed the shape of his head to that of a teardrop.

'Bill,' a gravelly voice said.

'Hello?' Bill said with false cheer.

The man walked closer and pulled his hood down revealing a bald head with a light fuzz around the ear line. 'Pay the fucking Bill,' he said.

The man was familiar; his voice and his mannerisms all registered in Bill's memory, but didn't produce any connection immediately. He deduced that this man must have owed money to someone at some stage.

The man stopped. 'You don't remember me, do you?' he said. 'Ruined so many lives that you can't place the people that had to deal with the aftermath?'

Bill took his hands from his pockets in case he needed to defend himself. 'I'm sorry, I don't remember who you are.'

The man stepped closer and out of the shadows, pulling the hood from his head. His face was pale and his eyes had dark rings. 'Let me remind you,' he said. 'You came to my place of business and demanded the money I owed.'

Bill didn't speak. One of the lessons he'd learned from doing his job was that there is a trigger point for every man that breaks the resolve. This conversation seemed to have started at that point. Bill thought about Charlie and Sully, wishing they were nearby. They would know what to do. Charlie always knew what to do.

'I'm sorry,' Bill said. 'I was just doing my job.'

The man yelled at him, 'So was I. So was I. Do you know who I am yet? Do you remember me?'

Bill shook his head, 'No, I'm sorry.'

'They used to call me Tony the Trigger.'

Bill remembered. Tony the Trigger was the first 'client' that Bill had dealt with after he'd been loaned out to other organisations. Tony the Trigger was the one who had started it all. Bill's mind raced. Why was Tony here now? All the way out here on the dock. How did he know Bill would be out here tonight? Bill hadn't even known *he'd* be out here tonight.

'What do they call you now?' Bill said, buying some time.

'What do they call me ... are you trying to be funny? Are you fucking with me, you fucking giant simpleton? They don't call me at all anymore. You ruined all that, you scumbag.'

Bill was taken aback. The hate Tony directed at him was blistering, as though the malice in the words was being thrown at him like darts piercing his skin. 'I'm sorry, I-I don't know what …' He stopped short. Tony was pointing a small revolver at his chest.

'Yeah, that's right. Do you remember me now, Bill? You showed up at my place of business. That hoity-toity brought you in so he didn't have to get his hands dirty. You are a fucking servant of the rich.'

Bill nodded. That was a fairly accurate description of Bill's role. He accepted that.

Tony went on, 'And do you remember my brother? The poor fucker you pulled out from behind the filing cabinets? Well, they cut his fucking fingers off.'

Bill gasped. 'What? Why?'

Tears glistened under Tony's red eyelids. 'So he couldn't point a shotgun at any more hoity-toity gangster bosses. All of them – cut them all off.'

'I didn't know,' Bill said. 'What can I do?'

'What can you *do*? Fuck me, Bill, you have already done it. You are good at what you do. Really fucking good. I paid the money back with interest. I told them they could leave us alone now. And you know what my brother did?'

Bill shook his head, appalled at what was happening and the fact he couldn't control it.

'He pulled the trigger one more time, even though he had no fingers on either hand. He was a clever dick, my brother. He got the shotgun down, put it in his mouth and pulled the trigger with his fucking toe. Ha. He showed them. He put another hole in the roof.'

'I—'

Tony pulled the trigger ... twice. The bullets entered Bill like hot knives. He stumbled backwards as pain rocked through his body. There was an odd sensation – as though things were loose inside him.

'I still have all my fingers, Bill; what I don't have is my brother. I don't have anything else either. My business is gone. My reputation is shot. My wife left with my kids. I don't even know where they are. So, Bill, thanks to you being good at your job, I'm totally fucked. Thank you, you cocksucker.'

Tony fired twice more.

Bill's knees buckled, and he fell backwards on his arse. The pain in his stomach flattened him onto his back. His head came to rest on the pylon. Bill's lungs weren't working. Breathing hurt. He coughed and tasted blood.

Tony hovered over him and smiled. 'Yeah, I got you, you prick.'

Bill squinted up at him, waiting for the final shot. The kill shot. But Tony kept talking. 'Yeah, Tony the Trigger.' He placed the end of the gun in his mouth and waved at Bill with the other hand. He stood straight and looked out to the darkness and waved again. He fired the revolver upwards into his brain. Tony the Trigger swivelled on his feet and fell, hitting the ground hard.

Bill looked up at the stars. He tried to move, but his body wasn't listening. He coughed and spat blood. A plane flew overhead, strobes flashing – an imitation star. Weakness flooded through him. He coughed again and a spear of pain electrified him. Fuck! He wasn't ready to die, not now, not tonight, goddammit. Just one more night, just give him this one night. Was someone coming? Was that a footstep he heard? He wanted to speak to Agatha, tell her something important but couldn't remember what. And he needed to pass a message on to Charlie and Sully. He wanted to let them know … what? He wasn't sure. Did he want to thank them? He wanted to say goodbye, that's what he wanted. He just wanted to talk to someone, anyone … one more time.

THE END.

www.ingramcontent.com/pod-product-compliance
Lightning Source LLC
Chambersburg PA
CBHW060514280326
41933CB00014B/2968